"Brandon Som celebrates his Chinese and Mexican ancestries by amplifying not collision but coalition—a cultural partnership that's existed in the Americas for generations, though seldomly encountered in poetry. At this vibrant intersection of language, ethnicity, and identity, inventive imagery is borne and so too a surprising lens that leaves us awestruck by Som's rich poetic landscape and multivalent story." —RIGOBERTO GONZÁLEZ, author of *To the Boy Who Was Night: New and Selected Poems*

"In *Tripas*, a vision of the self is profoundly contingent on portraits of others that manifest 'what's passed down, what's recovered.' Som brings a consciousness of 'tenor & rasp' to poems informed by family gossip and social history, one's place of origin and one's place of immigrant footing, and the textures of Chinese and Spanish. Saturated with exuberant language and story, the poems in *Tripas* have the amplitude of archives and the intimacy of songs." —RICK BAROT, author of *The Galleons*

"'What is it we keep? What is obsolete?' *Tripas* shows us the insides of conversations, family lineage, and technological objects as a line in itself—everything connected— the wires, the 'piecework,' the harmonics of English, Spanish, and Chinese, and the people in his family whose labor and language are tied and inextricably linked to material and matter. As the daughter of a microchips assembly-line worker, I have been waiting for this book from the grandson of a Motorola plant worker, and I see how these poems are fragments that are not fractured, but found, heard, recorded. Som's poems are a ledger of love that shifts, traces, extends that which telephones often do: split distance and cut across time to bring us closer to what is created." —JANICE LOBO SAPIGAO, author of *Microchips for Millions*

Tripas is a beautiful book and a wondrous reading experience. It transcends multiple borders, telling vivid family stories in gorgeous lyrical language. Whether honoring his Chinese grandfather or Chicana nana or other colorful characters—the poems flow euphonically line to line, with fine phrasing and deep compassion. . . . If personal is universal, this family portrait represents the beauty and resiliency of our diverse and colorful human condition. It augurs a spectacular world to come." —MARILYN CHIN, author of *A Portrait of the Self as Nation: New and Selected Poems*

T0026623

TRIPAS

Georgia Review Books   EDITED BY Gerald Maa

TRIPAS

POEMS BY Brandon Som

The University of Georgia Press *Athens*

Published by the University of Georgia Press
Athens, Georgia 30602
www.ugapress.org
© 2023 by Brandon Som
All rights reserved
Designed by Erin Kirk
Set in Garamond Premier Pro

Most University of Georgia Press titles are
available from popular e-book vendors.

Printed digitally

Library of Congress Control Number: 2022945665
ISBN: 9780820363509 (paperback)
ISBN: 9780820363516 (epub)
ISBN: 9780820363585 (PDF)

for Nana Pastora

in memory of

my father
Ng Ng
Yeh Yeh
& Tata Chickie

CONTENTS

TRIPAS

They say her cry is heard near water. My nana says she heard the story first as a child & then years later, on the line at Motorola, from a woman raised near Bisbee. Chismes y dichos—hearsay, as they inspected the endless circuitry through microscopes. Fordism's orders, overseers & foremen told her they would make phones that fit inside a pocket.

¡Yo no lo creía! If we remove their cases, the verbs *creer* & *to create* share similar wiring. Some of those components were washed, degreased, with toxic solvents—trichloroethylene—that Motorola for years spilled & flushed carelessly. A plume of poisoned groundwater stretches beneath Phoenix from the east valley to the west, past downtown where my father ran his store, a tiendita called Fay's, but that many knew as los chinos. After a nine-year fight with cancer, my father passed away in 2018.

In 1989, Motorola moved the production line my nana worked on to Mexico, once the company was served with fines for what's now a Superfund site. We might trace this production line from Phoenix, to Guadalajara, to subsidiaries in Guangzhou, where my father's family emigrated from—first my Yeh Yeh in the twenties & later my Ng Ng & Ai Gu in 1948, the year the first transistor was invented. I might hear in that technology my family's song, in broken pieces, bits of gossip like a game of telephone or Chinese whispers—*your own, your own*, cries Llorona from those little phones inside our pockets.

ONE

Are we are the letters, Mamita? Óyeme, are we are the ones
inside the words?

—JUAN FELIPE HERRERA

Cómo se dice, my circuitry, sews me—me cose—
word by word & dictates—how do you say?
 She translates, wires me, rewires rosary—*Rosario*
was my mom's name, she tells me. Decades pray me
an aria con cuerdas—como Ariadne. My dark moles,

 she says, are lunares. I think astronaut, a May moon
at perigee. There's lightning in the Chinese電,
 but I see lasso & chain link in the componentry,
 an analemma tracing dagongmei & ensambladoras
from rural town to city factory. In my browser today,

 feminists in China elude censors with rice
& bunny emoji for 'mi' 'tu' resistance. I hear the motorcycle
 revving within Nana's ándale but need to sound
out jíjole in my Anzaldúa so sound meets memory.

> *everyone*
> *take*   *gold*
> *a*   *mountain*
> *look*   *ship*

Ng Ng's postcard read when she came with Ai Gu
in 1948. A mountain inside our paper-name,
 there's gold in the pun. Great-grandfather—learning
 my grandfather used papers for his daughter—
scolded, "More money in sons!" Nana, for my poem,

gave me her pliers—green handle, needle nose—
a finer pair of fingers to tweeze semiconductors—
        wafer after wafer. Her niños—years later, my tías & tíos—
    home from elementary, helped straighten the leads—
pulling pigtails of transistors, leaping code switches

    & warming tortillas. Oír origins—an echo in the hecho.
Xicana Cherríe Moraga writes about her mother's
        "piecework"—how she sat nightly before the TV,
    "wrapping copper wires into the backs of circuit boards."
Braiding, I think, to parse & plait the wires that lit

    the images she watched. I looked up in Cosmo
that knot work—French, Dutch, Fishtail, Braid-to-Bun,
        Milkmaid & Halo—those chongos Nana made—
    the yank & tugged-tie, the brushwork through
the dark hair of daughters that often sparked.

CHINO

The olla knocked with steam. The masa cooked.

She said her eyes are china. The vowel switched
on an aura, a shine that sheens the threshold.

The vowel was spell: an *i* that might *we*,
an *i* that echoes how we're seen & see.

*Eye*dentity. Ay Dios, she exclaimed,
surrounded by photos—niños & nietos—

where I'm the only chino. How might I
see through my family's eyes—an owl's eyes

in ojos & one in its lid turned sideways 目 —
I wondered with her at the table where we

placed one olive—ojo negro—in each hoja,
that worn folio for field corn's field notes.

What does that dark eye in the ear's husk see?

RASPADAS

A keening sent
           throughout
      Barrio Campito,
                Nana Chayo's grinder
crushed block ice
      for her raspadas.

Just west
           of stockyard
      slaughter & Union
                Pacific tracks, she
too conducted
      that silver arm,

in her home's
           small storefront,
      feeding ice
                to shaving teeth.
In *raspar*,
      hear her voice's

saw-scratch

               & wood fire below

     enameled pots.

                     Ronco—my nana,

her daughter, says

     when I call up

enfermo. Like bronco

               & bronchitis & those

     roping winds

                     in mesquite—

open opera,

     these trees hoarse

with asthma.

               Huelga came too

     from pant, blow

                     & breathe. Bellows

resist, so in '72

     when Huerta

    & Chávez came

                to Campito

        for his fast

          at Santa Rita Hall

that summer,

        amid monsoon

no less, they chanted

                with Coretta Scott King

       & Joan Baez

                        sí se puede

across the street

        from my nana's tiendita

y raspadas.

                Con leche, con piña,

      con fresa,

                    she poured flavors

from bottles

        lit like church glass.

Up from Sinaloa,
                    1917, she came bird
          breasts to her
                                breasts, bra-pinioned
wings,
          smuggling swaddled-tight

cockatoos
                    silenced over the
          border
                                with coos & seed.
Rosario, entrepreneur,
          renter of tar roofs

to gold-toothed
                    cattlemen,
          stood over pit-fire
                                ladling to sod farmers
tripe & hominy,
          & started out, some

years prior,
                    from lettuce cars
          packed, bound
                                for markets east,

swiping ice cakes
        for her raspadas—

their bright rosary
                our heirloom. Went by
      Chayo for short.
                        Rancheras from her radio—
I saw her once
      shake out her dress & molt.

MY TATA, MY LI PO

The poems, then, are those of a man who in the eyes of a society
largely dominated by bureaucratic values had completely failed in
his career or rather had failed to have a career at all.

—ARTHUR WALEY

Li Po of loppers, extension cords & carpenter's pants—
hammer's claw snug in its loop. Li Po of roach clips,
porno mags, his Ziplock of batteries. Li Po licking each

nipple to test its charge. Li Po of Thunderbird,
of Night Train—winito stash—in the piñon's knothole
for his night sips. Li Po of Korean War—*I joined*

to see the world, he once said, *but they sent me*
to Albuquerque. He learned his drink in basic training,
Nana says. Li Po of government checks, of Hohokam

acequias instead of any Yangtze. Li Po of swollen
knuckles from nuns' rulers for speaking his Spanish.
Li Po of turn around & net snap. Li Po of s-hooks,

where crescent wrenches hung like caught fish.
Li Po of cuidados & chingados. The rascuache Li Po
of cochinero, of makeshift. Li Po of Saltillo tiles,

terracotta—tierra mía—awaiting square feet.
Li Po, who quizzed me, call & response, *Do you know*
your times? I know my times, Li Po. Li Po of the x,

the unknown, the adopted, the *indio*, the crossing
& extension of dimensions. X the Spanish borrowed
from the Greeks when translating the Arabic integer

of Al Jebr, that system "reconciling the disparate parts,"
that calculus of Mexica in Xicano. Li Po of loose
timing belts & palomas in bougainvillea. Li Po, claro,

of moons, the one bitten to the quick, or slightly
bigger—a potter's rib scraping something from nothing.
Li Po of aloe & layups. Li Po of scrap metal, miscut

lumber saved for the day when you needed them—
his futurism. Li Po in that army photo with his best Jorge
Negrete moustache. Though I can't see his wrist,

the watch is wound & I still hear the second hand
sucking its teeth. Li Po of VFW all-touch bank shots.
Li Po of Pachuco & morning knuckle pushups.

OVERDUB

In the movie, the one-armed boxer, in order to teach his students
    balance, walks the rim of a rush basket. His judicious

steps never overturn or buckle the thin,

wicker mouth. The temple pupils express awe—overdubbed
    with an English, more or less than

their lips' shape. In one memory, I am again before my tío's
    posters of Bruce Lee & with a reverence often reserved

for cave painting or ancient scrolls. I was disciple,

learning what roughhousing made of home: *cojones, más macho, more*
    beans—my tío taunted to toughen me. Hardly fury, fists small

as limes, I mimed the blows by nunchucks in a dresser mirror,
    where nightly he hung his gold chain & crucifix—

a First Communion gift. Listen. Can you hear Tío, just a teen,
    say his *Our Father* before bed while behind him

Bruce Lee, in a many-mirrored chamber, stood

open-mouthed with kung fu cry? In the movie's penultimate scene,
    the one-armed fighter lures his blind nemesis

into an aviary, hoping to employ birds

to ransack his enemy's heightened hearing. With all the cage doors
   open, the sound is wing-flight & coo

amid their kicks & punches.

CLOSE READING

forest selva 林

—FRANCES CHUNG

One for *tree*, two for *woods*,

      Ai Gu wrote the characters

木 林

      out for me. Dehiscent & reminiscent:

what wood made

      Ng Ng's hope chest

that she immigrated with

      —cargo from Guangzhou

to Phoenix? In Spanish, Nana tells me,

      hope & waiting are one word.

————

In her own hand, she keeps

      a list of dichos—*for your poems*, she says.

Están más cerca los dientes

      que los parientes, she recites her mother

& mother's mother. *It rhymes*, she says.

      Dee-say—the verb with its sound

turned down looks like dice,
        to throw & dice, to cut. Shift after shift,

she inspected the die of integrated circuits
        beneath an assembly line of microscopes—

the connections over time
        getting smaller & smaller.

———

To enter words in order to see
—Cecilia Vicuña

In the classroom, we learn iambic words
        that leaf on the board with diacritics—

about, aloft, aggrieved. What over years *accrues*

within one's words? What immanent
        sprung with what rhythm?

Agave—a lie in the lion, the maenad made mad,

by Dionysus, awoke to find her son
        dead by her hand. The figure is gaslit

even if anachronistic. Data & riverbanks—
        memory's figure is often riparian.

I hear La Llorona's agony echo
        in the succulent. What's the circuit in cerca

to short or rewire
        the far & close—to map
                Ng Ng & Ai Gu to Nana's carpool?

———

I read a sprig of evergreen, a symbol
        of everlasting, is sometimes packed

with a new bride's trousseau. It was thirteen years

before Yeh Yeh could bring
        Ng Ng & Ai Gu over. Evergreen

& Empire were names of corner stores

where they first worked—
        stores on corners of Nana's barrio.

Chinito, Chinito! *Toca la malaca*—
        she might have sung in '49

after hearing Don Tosti's
        recording—an *l* where the *r* would be

in the Spanish rattle filled with beans or seed or as
        the song suggests

change in the laundryman's till.

I have read diviners
        use stems of yarrow when consulting
                the I-Ching.

What happens to the woods in a maiden name?

Two hyphens make a dash—
        the long signal in the binary code.

Attentive antennae: a monocot

—seed to single leaf—the agave store years
        for the stalk. My two grandmothers:

one's name keeps a pasture,
        the other a forest. If they spoke to one another,

it was with short, forced words
        like first strokes when sawing—

                trying to set the teeth into the grain.

FUCHI

Fuchi when we passed the stockyard
or city incinerator. *Who threw a fart,*
Nana would ask, as if the offense
were a grenade or football. I didn't know
the origins of her phrase, its handoff,
until I learned *tirar* in Spanish class.
I've read of toxins in electronics plants—
chemicals that poison, cause cancers,
numb the senses of smell & taste
with odors in so-called clean rooms.
Did the smells elicit a fuchi? Fool please,
I hear in the word. I hear Chinese too.
Think of those moves in Qi Gong—
part the horse's mane, strum the lute,
grasp the sparrow's tail. Could they ward
off cancers? Release toxins? Repair
one's chi after one's shift? I remember
watching Chi Chi Rodríguez parry
his putter with a flourish after sinking
a put, then sheath the club at his waist
in a make-believe scabbard. In grad school,
I learned of Kristeva's abject, those
liminal spaces between what we reject
& what we obsess. Growing up chino,
the question I was most often asked,
besides what are you, was *do you know
kung fu. Kung*, I looked up, means
skillful work, hard training, or endeavor.

Fu means time spent. I ask my nana
about her time in the factory. *I worked
the scopes,* she says, *looking for marks.
If the wafer was scratched, I threw it out.*
What is it we keep? What is obsolete?
*That's when I think my eyes started
to go bad.* What kind of seeing is hard-
wired in our circuitry? *They were
like tiny little maps,* she tells me, *of the city.*

The -ah was more song
& she sang beyond the name.
If the name were river,
the -ah flooded its banks.
Nonetheless, in its song
the -ah signed the air,
made the air mean.
The -ah hitched & hinged
its intimacy. Jaw-dropped,
it crooned its diminutive—
sang of class, filling
a back kitchen at lunch
where a wok clangs
& a knife trims the gristle.
In the stockroom with her,
it kept accounts, was ledger,
an idea of order among
Schlitz & Old Milwaukee.
From tones in the pharynx,
from lungs that hung
like two clipboards,
came the -ah's inventory.
She tied the -ah to my name
like that old trick—
tongue-tying cherry stem.
Quipu or rosary,
in the knot was knowing.

She threaded the eye to sow
a threnody. Liturgy, the way
she sang the vowel
amid the till bell—
a field song over produce.
A nah, a nope, or uh-oh,
it was abracadabra,
an endnote, a colophon
bearing the binder's mark.
It lingered incarnate
in the cold walk-in
or ghosted the stocked aisles
where I stood over cans
of Ajax & Green Giant.
The -ah was wavelength,
a frequency shape
like a mountain range.
It was the gesture's aura,
& like a varnish
it lustered my name
& diminished like a mark
in the margin. It was whistle house,
a star's spur, & it could scold
from the meat counter,
where she priced the chuck
with a grease pen tied to the scale.
In her long breath, the -ah
was money to burn,
incense in a Folgers can.

In the ear, as if in a mirror,
I found myself listening
& like all language
it was a grave's treats,
singing of separateness
& tracing something complete.
Though not on a map
its lilt echoed the geographies
& she hummed it
simply over a thin broth,
simmered daylong
& suckled on a short rib.

TWO

if the codes make us complicit

—JANICE LOBO SAPIGAO

I Google & get gemela but know cuate from coatl: the twin & serpent
entwined in the word—

> mirror image of head
> > & tail, forked tongue knit
> of sibling & sibilance.

In *Maquilapolis*, without the factory parts, the women workers in Tijuana
mime for the camera. They could be tethering distant kites, leading
discrete symphonies, churning arms in tai chi's cloud hands, rather than
assembling

> flat screens for a factory plant.
> *Move your hands as fast as your mouths,*

my nana says her supervisor ordered them in Phoenix. She started in '68,
her line work that moved duty-free parts from factory to fábrica, over the
border, to be assembled with cheaper labor. Retiring in the nineties, as
the murders of maquila workers were on the rise, my grandmother may
have had a part, a chip she inspected, placed inside a product by a woman
working in Juárez.

Faced with the violence, words seem empty, feel fabricated. When I try
imagining the woman holding the circuit my grandmother inspected, I
am shy & frightened. Maybe she came up to the border from Durango or
Oaxaca, maybe Sinaloa, where my nana's mom, Rosario, came up from.
Maybe, like her, it was the first time leaving home. I imagine parts of a life
but cannot know the whole.

In Spanish class, we learn indirect & direct object pronouns, how they connect to the conjugated verb. In English, I place

> the who before whom
> > & what in the wake of acts.
> To think of indirect

& direct in union with my actions is to think in relation. In the syntax of an assembly line—what part of speech are you? What part is duty-free?

I like to imagine the talk & clap back, the factory line side-eye somehow encoded on those Phoenix circuits—recorded, overdubbed, downloaded within

> the photolithographic
> > nano-paths my nana Pat

& her coworkers inspected. Lithography originally copied sheet music. Could we then hear a choir—a gossip of warning, of healing, of organizing & resistance—inscribed on the staff lines of the circuit?

Chisme is gossip but also gadget, the thingamajig, from Latin's cimex, that bug

> & malware of whisper,
> > hack of na-huh,
> & virus of ¿de veras?

on a circuitry neither discrete nor discreet but integrated with words and like the phones their parts made

moving at light speeds & faster
than their hands ever could.

I am sitting with mermaids of the air—
their fishtails from a monger's stall, where they
were lifted from ice bed to butcher's block
& wrapped in newsprint. Now they type
over carriage & keys, these two sirens
& their Olivetti. I imagine the photographer
reading Homer & considering how in both
inspiration & temptation we encounter
a beseeching or thinking that the mermaids,
with their knowledge of tides & the late
summer's phosphorescence, might say something
about the startling beauty of betweenness.
My father, born in '51 in Phoenix, once found
with me on the dim sum's placemat his rabbit sign.
Jackrabbit, I think now—so called for its
long ears similar to a pack donkey. Scrubland
critter beneath prickly pear. A sage eater
preyed upon by hawk & harvester in the sod
& cotton fields outside Avondale, where my father
kept his shop. Then the char siu came, sliced
with its red edges like a kiss on a napkin.
I knew, of course, La Sirena on the lotería
that Nana called from the deck. With dried beans
for markers, we listened on the edge of bingo.
Afterward, we gathered each bean to cook
with garlic & salt, maybe a piece of saved fat
that simmered, as we slept, until morning,
when Nana would be returning from third shift.
Homer never describes the Sirens as sexy.

At other times in history, they are part bird
& not fish at all. Euripides lists them as servants
of Persephone, crossing between this world
& the next. The montage leaps with modernism's
mixing of perspectives, empire's far-flung
violence & fragmentation. Some say bingo
echoes a Cantonese word that asks who? Asks
which person? If Googled, *sirenas de aire*
shows us ads for air raid sirens. Can you see
my string of beans, its rosary of call & response
over images—so suddenly, so briefly—all in a row?

SHAINADAS

Ese Louie . . .
Chale, call me "Diamonds", man!
—JOSÉ MONTOYA

Tata shined shoes
as a boy for movie money
& I imagined how

a shine box might fit
under the theater's seat
the way it fit decades

later when I saw it
in that dark beneath
my grandparent's old,

sunken spring-bed.
Later bulldozed,
the Phoenix theater

must have looked
like those prewar
cinemas mostly lost

now but documented
in the photographs
of Hiroshi Sugimoto—

for which the artist
placed his large-
format camera

in the last rows
of spring-shut seats
below ornate

wall carvings
& baroque sconces,
where he then

left the camera's
aperture open
for a full feature.

It is what we see
of stars—all endings
& untouchable

beginnings: images,
characters & plot
gone & only white

light left. The cedar box
housing brushes,
rags & tins of polish

had its hinged latch
& the handle that
also cradled a shoe.

My foot's never
touched it, but I wonder
which brush inside

might brush back,
against the grain,
one of those photos,

to extend the wet
finger of projection
over a boy who

looks up toward
the screen like he looked
up from a shine.

Or is the figure
to borrow from that
other invention?

Could I carve open
a pinhole in the shine box
for its storehouse

of inverted images?
—as if revolutions were that
simple an apparatus

of optics to have
the shiner ascend there
to what shines.

CYPHER

Breaking, my cousin Alex
made his belly wave in series
by force like gravity,
made a sea on his stomach
rip curl, made a moon
over his breaking boy's body.
A Phoenix kid, he was waves
in a desert like dunes wave
out west on 8, past Yuma,
or like the screen waves
on the machines his mom, Chita,
monitored for Motorola.
His was all stomach, his panza
formed like that word
from morning's sweet rolls.
He would lift his shirt to show
the circle, to say step off,
to throw shade or gauntlet,
to lay down the law or say can't
touch this with his walk-off
swan song, his ace, his go-to.
He'd lift his shirt like elders do
for a breeze on lunch breaks,
to let skin in day's heat breathe
& let their gut rest, let gut go
be full, round; or at home
once a work day's done—
cold can on gut's curve, its crest,

to let the can sweat there now
instead of them. Indeed, he'd dance
where they sometimes drank—
VFWs or Legions. In veteran places
where first communions or
quinceañeras happen, they would
robot, centipede, helicopter,
moonwalk—as if those moves
were earth science classes.
In fact, his stomach translated,
transduced—his textbook told him—
the deejayed sound: sound's wave
made flesh, sound incarnate.
On a belly where shipmates
might tattoo, turning needles
from their scrimshaw, his stomach
was canvas to sine & cosine,
rise over run he might've graphed
on a TI-81—the way they sign
whale song. A verse, flesh scrolled
a phone's text before phones
rolled like that. There we stood,
cousins, some dressed for catechism
to receive sacrament. Our awes
made moons on our faces
as he popped & locked—his gold
chain with the crucifix safely
in his lips while he lifted his shirt
simple-like, as if undressing for bed.

QINGMING

At his register, my father kept a ballpoint
for IOUs & cashed checks tucked
behind his ear. What's that thin space called?
Arroyo & hair barrette, holster & small
bud vase; its clasp sometimes a clothespin
to a cigarette, those loosies Eric Garner
allegedly sold outside a corner store
like my dad's, outside the state-taxed hard
& soft packs I kept stocked, as a kid,
in their display case, their columned rows
an abacus above us. I go to my dad's gravestone
in its granite row of grocer's graves
saying Harlins, saying Garner, saying Floyd,
kowtowing with tin-foiled dumplings
in the spirit smoke of burning ghost money,
those twenties my dad held to the light
for their watermark, despite the counterfeit
of our paper name—its papel picado,
& IOU, its side hustle & shortchange.
Corners are spaces with angles, spaces
with edges. I remember my father bowlegged
behind his push broom or leaning back
a dolly of Modelo & Mickeys to truck
the store rows, to stock the cold reach-in.
Though I didn't know it then, I was learning
the paper in all names: the pulp & slur
of syllables, how they keep a silence even as
you say them. Better to hear match strike
& scratch-tickets, as I sweep the inextricable,

the fricatives of those chiseled characters
my dad couldn't read but that scroll on the stone
like his register's receipts. Better to listen
inside those unnamable spaces that call in
our dead, who ask that we do more than grieve.

TATTOO

Soy un amasamiento, I am an act of kneading...
—GLORIA ANZALDÚA

Her hermanos' manos had *maseros*
tattooed in the half-moon between
thumb & finger—written in India ink,
the word green like a hand's vein
—as if blood swelled to cursive
their gang name. *Fíjate, they had those*
tattoos when we buried them, she says—
corn silk on husking hands, her rings
& bracelets beside the kneading bowl.
Her abuelos in the barrio Cuatro Milpas,
like the ranchera, tended field corn,
she tells me, for their tienda: sowers
beside a scarecrow that I imagine
was broom spine & segunda sweater—
secondhand in their sowers' hands:
what's passed down, what's recovered.
Sold masa, she says, from horse-cart,
harvested stalks after their first silk,
peeled from ears the leaves to lay out—
their green yellowing in the day's heat
—& then simmered the shelled grain
in a wood ash lye for the nixtamal—
a Nahuatl word with ash in the root
as if the word were recipe or how-to.
Without her brothers' hands to read,

I look for their word but only find
the feminine *masera*, a kneading trough;
& its homophone *macero*, mace bearer—
European figure of power, symbol
of rule. I cannot speak in Spanish
the difference between the two—
can't say masa without mace's trace,
a hiss that can't hush its violence.
How might it sound a resistance too?
I've brought a map to ask about
those barrios along Buckeye before
all was bought out. El Campito,
her hood, where the train tramps
camped under mesquite—*we drew lines,*
she says, *in the dirt beneath them for rooms*
to play house. Sectioned, I thought,
like las milpas & her abuelos' work
plowing their parcel—the barrio's
furrows like the conjunto's accordion:
its bellows crop lines, song-citing
larger histories of upheaval & loss.
We read of redlining & covenants
that kept neighborhoods Anglo only.
Fíjate, she says otra vez—this time
to punctuate. Though I've heard it
all my life, I have to look it up too,
to spell it: from the transitive
to fix, to stick up or on, take notice.
Listen, can you believe it, check it out,
go figure, isn't it something, the word slips
despite its definition, its fixation.

Fíjate, we wore finger cots on the line,
rubbers on our fingers. They didn't want
our prints on the electronics. Fíjate,
I had a friend in that white neighborhood.
We would play. Once she had me over
for dinner. I'll never forget. She told me,
I'm going to eat like you. *Like me?*
I thought. Then I saw what she meant.
She used her bread to eat with her fingers.
Dough makers with tally sheets
—ranchers paid with chickens—
sometimes cow's milk—maseros writes
against the miscounting sounded
out in the word. Its script, rivering
like the Salt did, traced them subjects
& subject to industry: stockyard,
meatpacking, & rendering. *Fíjate,*
they called us greasers. Addendum or
annotation, their *maseros* revised
the sentence written on their body.
I carry that archive—what's stored
without inventory: a leaf, an aleph;
a casita in husk; a feminine eye inside
hoja; maize, maíz, masa—a maze
on fingertips. Hear the word again—
at its center a gristmill of cicada,
a mesquite both vessel & wishbone.

The physicist Faraday drew "lines of force"
with iron filings, lithe as eyelashes, across
the waxed paper he set atop bar magnets.
A chiaroscuro, the diagram connects the dots
to those homing birds with beaks that act
as lodestones. One of the two characters
in the Chinese word for compass has a net
for catching birds. With only the papers
for Colombia, the number-four son made
a plan with his older brother, the oldest
of that generation, a sojourner who settled
down in the States. The younger brother
would take a flight with a layover in Phoenix,
where a doctor, the family knew, could
diagnose him with some medical excuse.
They chose an ear infection. The Latin sews
together with *step* or *pace*. Charging one
ion, we compass compassion. What wires
a poem's enjambment, its bandwidth between,
like a field of hidden ribbon? Their plan
didn't work. My uncle spent four years
in back kitchens in Bogotá learning Spanish
before his English, which he pieced together
eventually back in Phoenix working the line
at Motorola—same plant my nana worked
with her perfect attendance. They never met.
What diagrams me—Malinchino, Pochinero,
Xicanese? A knockoff from open sources,
makeshift & hacked from component bins.

Chop suey, that all-American dish, means
"mixed pieces." I imagine them passing now
& then in the break room or at the time clock.
The inner ear is also called the labyrinth.
It contains the cochlea—little snail shell
or screw—& that network of boney canals
essential for balance. In the Western myth
the quills are dipped in wax, like wax were ink
—as if to write *wing*. Was that labyrinth's
design based on the human ear? The echo
in the hecho would suggest endless sources,
"byzantine supply chains." Oreja of course
is the Spanish. I hear its *or* & think of sound
as a series of alternatives—a kind of hyphen
-omenology: how within parallel circuits
currents increase across increased resistance.

She starts to tell me about a father she didn't know,
how the barrio did though & called her Nehi
   on account of his truck—its stained-glass payload
  of soda pop—parked those afternoons out front

  her mother's tienda. She says his name, that he was Filipino,
before adding, *I'm half like you, mijo.* In poems, we learn
   to call a rhyme that isn't true, half or slant. Slant-eyed,
  a slur, what half-rhymes do she & I make?

  Two makes your five & five makes your ten. His hands out
& thumb wet, my father laid the bills down to teach me
   to count change back. Above him, in Phoenix heat,
  a light snow fell on the harnessed Clydesdales

  inside a Bud sign. Of hawkers' songs & storekeepers' chants,
we might imagine those in the stalls of cobbled shoes,
   barreled pulque & bolts of cloth; before the weaver's
  spinning wheel or a nevería's flasks of sweetened syrup—

  in the 18th century's casta paintings inscribing mixed races
within Enlightenment thinking: its genocide & chattel slavery,
   its blood math & market goods. What of those ledgers
  figures our halfness inside her Phoenix kitchen?

  In fridge light or bent down to blow range gas back
to the pilot, hands slick with the Morrell Snow Cap
   greasing the lucent Pyrex, how are we half or wholly
  in those canvases still? Or my father at his register

crooning his math, singing the infinite divisions. *No Te Entiendo*, reads the inscription for a mixing too difficult

to determine. The pun of *half* & *have* cuts with the ache of never enough. Does knowing where the halfing starts

bring us closer to whole? I see my father still in a swaying two-step over the meat slicer, his right hand beneath

butcher paper held out almost lovingly, as if cradling someone's head & not just catching slices of ham.

THREE

We might hope to find the three activities—poetry, science, politics—triangulated, with extraordinary electrical exchanges moving from each to each and through our lives.

—ADRIENNE RICH

ANTENNA

Tuning not lute but car radio, Cocteau's Orpheus
copies the broadcasts from a netherworld for verses—

his muse a circuitry my grandmother inspected

nights at Motorola. Before her shift, she put me to bed,
laid down beside me & smoked Parliaments—

each drag like tower light to planes overhead.

From crest to crest is wavelength & frequency
the number per second. Where the waves won't reach,

we call shadow, count the radio's components

like prosody—diodes, triodes, tetrodes—& dial
the frequency in meters. Jack Spicer cited quasars,

quasi-stellar radio traveling lightyears, as possible sources.

I remember Orion—one slick matador, Tió called him
—up on South Mountain, leaning on towers,

red-eyed with warning & somehow—by frequency,

by transmissions I vaguely knew—drunk with music.
With ham operator, Pauline Oliveros sent a *hello*

to the moon's tympanum. It bounced back, dropped

in pitch by Doppler effect & she accompanied
the sound on accordion. A nana is lullaby, cradlesong,

I tell my mom, a nana now & we talk about how

neither of us had heard that before: canción de cuna—
the lacuna we hum (& tune by)—its tonic note

a chord knot we worry (& teethe on) with night song.

One grandmother with Vicks, one with Tiger Balm,
rubbed fires of camphor & mint, old poultices,

into my chest: their palms kneading & wet with salve,

its menthols, to strip the chaff & rattle in a night wheeze.
Can you hear their lullabies? One like the dicho,

chiquito pero picoso, one in all five tones of village dialect—

with wish-hum for thresholds, they put to bed each name
for the night. In Cocteau's version, Orpheus crosses

over through a tailor's mirror. The carnival house optics

of Marx's commodity fetish, I thought, or my father
in Phoenix, stocking the reach-in with Old Milwaukee

& seeing in the glass, a brief moment, his own reflection.

Ai Gu tells me great-grandfather frequented Chinatown
fortune-tellers, ones with charts & calendars—a crystal-ball

almanac for a paper son on a paper path, a celestial

divination in the back room of butcher or herbal shop,
or corner store like our own, where till bell drifted back

to find Ng Ng—her wok kicking spark off stove flame—

or find me at a desk my father fashioned from Schlitz
twelve-packs for weekend's homework: me copying out

my name—a dotted line running through its center—

& not knowing the silences, not knowing then the cost
of turning back to see. In today's news, U.S. troops install

the miles of border razor wire, so-called concertina

for the coil that extends & flattens like the bellows
of a squeeze-box. "Listen to everything all the time & remind

yourself when you are not listening," instructed Oliveros,

a composer of sonospherics & a chi kung student
of quantum physics. "In practicing," she once explained

"I have experienced listening with the palms of my hand."

RESISTORS

I just felt like he was fighting us with his machine.
—NELLIE JO DAVID

In Guadalajara to see where Motorola took the line
    my grandmother worked on, I can't find the site
but spend the days in naves of a deconsecrated church

looking up at frescoes by Orozco. Here is a horse:
    a tow chain for tail, train piston for hock & hoof.
Over murdered Mexica, Cortez stands: lug nut hips

& kneecaps, gauntleted hand at the sword hilt, silver
    as a knot of solder. Opposite him: the Franciscan
& his Latin cross—miter-sawed angles hewn down

to dagger point—& an angel in assembly-line armor
    lifting a bloodied banner with the stenciled letters
of an alphabet, the one I must have started learning,

sing-song in the pitch & timbre of milk teeth, at 48th
    & Willetta, a one-bedroom duplex west of Papago's
greasewood & buttes of sandstone & a block down

from the Motorola where my grandmother punched
    in nights to look after a conveyor of semiconductors—
those nascent ancient rotaries strung up to starlight

& empire (gaslighting like that Gast painting of progress
        & whiteness wrapped in telegraph wire, lithe & looping
as cake shop box string). *No wall on O'odham land,*

I hear the woman today protest from the bucket
        of a front-end loader—a Caterpillar, by her presence,
dumbstruck on tread wheels tall as vault doors, its maw

metal hollow, a confessional or old Mountain Bell
        phone booth she stepped into amid the felled saguaro
& ribs of organ pipe. Her body where dirt goes says

her body is the land the wall wants to eat. I stream this—
        download by data plan, by bandwidth, from the cloud
servers deep in their grid deserts to the crystalline

& rare earth minerals making my cell phone
        black box theater, making her code, making her
algorithm—both soprano & Mario Savio—the solder

seemingly quantum leap from soldada & solidarity.
        Still, I remember the ram's horn baritone in my nana's
King James, imagine her driving those years with riders

to shepherd the sound through solid state & know
        the harder truth: the defiant mic this woman makes,
resonates with her body beneath the digger's teeth.

MY FATHER'S PERM

He asked his younger brother
        —back from L.A.
    & recently out—
           to give it to him.

They took a dining
        room chair—
    cracked vinyl, chrome legs
           —into Ng Ng's kitchen

beside the sink
        where she washed her rice,
    hands pressed
        as if to pray

but with grains
        whispering instead
    between them. I was raised
        with two names for whiteness:

gringo & lo fan,
        white rice with dinner
    or morning jōk,
        runny with sausage.

In this picture,
        I must be three,
    maybe four. My folks then
        have just split up.

We lean into one another
                    —my bowl cut,
          his thin curls
                              almost pencil-drawn.

Chino in Spanish
                              also means curly.
          What did curls mean
                              after their divorce?

Like their failed marriage,
                    what racial lines
          was his new do crossing?
                              Was he watching

Black Panthers marching
                    in Oakland?
          Was he thinking about
                              Mom's brothers,

my tíos, a decade
                    after blowouts,
          blow-drying back
                              pompadours?

What might a permanent
                    have meant to him,
          son of a paper son
                              & shopkeeper?

What steadiness
        did he hope for
    more than a Quick-Stop
          when listening nights

to "Always & Forever"?
        Is it wrong to hear
    "Let's Stay Together"
          in that hot curl treatment

rinsed at a sink
        often filled with gai choy
    & cut onion
          from Ng Ng's garden?

She said she wouldn't go
        to the wedding, Mom says
    when I ask about
          those days. *She had old,*

traditional ways.
        I didn't fit. Maybe I saw
    her ways in furrows
          she labored—scarecrowed

with bow rake
        & whipping the hose free.
    Sowing here what
          she knew over there,

with jute bag

             of cabbage & lotus root,

     she reaped against

                 the loss. What did she think

of Uncle's perm rods

             beside her chopping block?

     I remember, Uncle texts,

                 dabbing where solution dripped

& burned down his neck.

             Solution suggests

     a problem's fixed. Standing over him—

                 Ng Ng's dishcloth

caped about his brother

             —my father's wet hair

     between his fingers,

                 Uncle rolled the curlers

giving my dad,

             we say *body*. In that moment,

     two bodies, two brothers—

                 a brother's hairdresser,

a brother's keeper—

             solve for the variables

     of desire & difference.

                 Her crossing irreducible

in the equation,

                Ng Ng swept up,

       I imagine, if any hair

                    was cut—bad luck

she would say,

              especially on New Year's,

     when cutting hair

                  is cutting one's fortune.

GRAMOPHONE

Sent across the Pacific with remittance
& with postcards of Roman arches,
Greek columns, flourishes of acanthus,
the Victor made in St. Louis—its horn
a thought bubble over the turntable—
sat in a Hoiping diaolou turned museum.
"Gramophone," read the curator's label
for us U.S.-born tourists. I looked up
the characters & found "song machine."
Curious mechanics, spinning's playback
as if song thread & singing a reeling
or unraveling. I see still spinning inside
quinceañera the small record player
Nana bartered from her mother in '49
rather than a party or new dress. I imagine
her dropping the 45s like a seamstress
does a bobbin. *They're here for you when
you're ready,* father said, packing &
alphabetizing his LPs—the subtext that
he wouldn't be. Phoenix-born in the '50s,
he didn't see China until his forties—
the age I am now, visiting for the first time,
our family village. Overlapped,
overdetermined—like I'm set in the groove
of one of his records. The week before
I left for China, I walked in Barrio Logan
with Day of the Dead processioners
beside the parked lowriders with popped
trunk altars—photos, velas, tequila

in tazas, serapes over a subwoofer's
low hum for loved ones. Behind the títeres,
we were led by the old skeletons—
Posada's etchings satirizing the white
& Western longings in our long
colonized closets. The cortege follows me,
a chino in China, where for twenty ren
I light incense in ancestral halls & recall
those last days feeding my bedridden
father his butter cookies & cold melon
while we listened to Redbone, the Chi-lites
& Temptations. His ofrenda might spin
Come & get your love or *Just my imagination*—
its gramophone's *song* made from *mouth*
& *gate*—the radical my dictionary tells me
could mean *entrance*, could mean *open ending*.

SUPER MERCADO LEE HOU

> Rather than a Chinatown, it looks like a rundown street where
> a few Chinese have dropped anchor, orphans of imperial dragons,
> thousand-year-old recipes, and mysteries.
> —RAFAEL BERNAL, *The Mongolian Conspiracy*

Amid the aisles of fideo
de huevo, de arroz,
hongo negro, shitake,
crisantemo, pétalo de lili
& clavo chino—
                    I remembered
how her apron pockets
kept a box cutter,
how she bagged Mad Dog
& Wild Turkey,
or wrapped precisely—
like a gift—a pig's foot
                    in wax paper.
In DF on Dolores Street
in barrio chino, south of South
Phoenix, Chinese grocers—
immigrants unassimilable
to the mixing in mestizaje—
sell spices & ingredients.
Curios too—palillos chinos,
ceramic conejos, dragones
de oro—like those in Borges's
compendium
                    of imagined beasts—

saddled by kings, the main
course of emperors—& beside
them were sobres rojos,
the lai see she wrote my Chinese
name on with a gung hay
fat choy, slipping inside good-
luck money. With hands
that punched at a register—
one-fingered like planting
seed in soil—those sheer hands
with barrettes or earwigs
pulled from the day's lettuce—
she wrote the strokes
that mirrored the thinness
of hand bones. I didn't know
the characters or luck
bought with their slice & sweep,
the spines of their first-
made marks.

          On envelopes
in ballpoint, the name
I couldn't sign but signed me
marked moon-phased
& moon-based New Year
in script that stayed ellipses
& recorded the paid
before I knew the received.

          On market signs
in Sharpie & Spanish
naming the "Products of China,"
we might read stevedores

on galleons, coolies of empire,
how the Chinese came
for centuries to Big Lusong.
Their descendants sold
sundries in the 1930s
in the copper towns of Sonora
before they were run out
by ordinance, by anti-chino
violence.
                    The same years,
under Hoover & so-called
repatriation, federal & state
agents searched payrolls
for Mexican-sounding names,
executing large-scale raids
that deported over a million
Mexican & Mexican Americans.
Could I sign my name
that crossing, that chiasmus
of exile, or simply share
a night's receipts—its archive
of saladitos, pack of Pall Malls,
tins of potted meat?
                    An IOU &
salt's cure, the longhand
she learned in a village schoolhouse—
long they say for long life,
long as glass noodles—keeps
sound & stores meaning,
writing in the margins or corners,
those tienditas de la esquina

where paths meet, or knot
like cut rope, or twist like those
figures of dragons.
                    "Inscrutable,"
Borges writes of their infinite
shapes & yet goes on with details
about claws, horns & scales,
their large horse—like heads
& snaking tail, the medicinal
uses of their teeth, how they keep
a pearl chained to their necks
& broil "whole shoals of fish"
with one breath, how one moves
like a river rising from earth,
its backbone bristling with spines.

TRANSMITTER

In Judy Baca's mural *The Great Wall,*
        a Chichimeca woman, on a comet tail
of field corn, hovers & whispers in the ear

of Edison, the Zacatecan, the secrets
        of the light bulb. Órale, my mom texts,
but autocorrect sends oracle instead.

I remember, as a kid, looking up from
        the passenger seat at the work badge
my grandmother after each shift clipped

to the rearview mirror's wood-bead rosary.
        A dashboard milagro in the dial light
of her Chevy, its toothed clasp bit into

the Hail Marys as if to test the solder
        of that circuitry. She often tells me
of Mexican movie stars—María Félix,

Jorge Negrete, Pedro Infante—how they
        toured the U.S. movie houses & signed
the ticket stubs she sold from a box office

skinny as a phone booth. A transmitter made
        from goldbeater's skin stretched across
a hoop drum, Bell's phonautograph

used pig bristle for a stylus to sign his
        speech waves on a plate of smoked glass.
I watched on YouTube Infante stand

with eleven mariachis, gallant in silk ties
        & epaulets, to serenade "Paloma"—
his tenor crooning about the unrequited man

turned dove with grief to the actress
        in bedclothes & bewitched as I imagine
Helmholtz, the pianist, holding a tuning fork

to an electromagnet & hearing it vibrate.
        Trying to picture that man wasting away
in heartache & so hollowed to bird bones

I reread this morning Socrates telling Phaedrus,
        outside the city walls of cicadas how they
were men before muses brought them song.

Unaware that cost, I climbed mesquite limbs
        for the discarded skins, brittle as chicharrones,
& cupped their match light in my boy hands.

Hearing, it's said, is touch at a distance.
        Ola is amp & trough. Frequency = waves
passing a given point. My nana's voice

is creosote & Parliaments—tenor & rasp
       that side-winds cell towers over chevrons
of ocotillo, through ironwood & arroyo,

moving in the megahertz her hands made.

NOVENA

And I pulled the cat's whisker,
rolled the coil in hope,
from my hands a phoenix fluttered—

—CHRISTOPHER GILBERT

A butcher's boy with oranges at the graves
        of Chinese launderers, takeout & liquor
    store owners, I'm awkward with kowtows
before the tombstone & old Folgers tin
        of lot sand & lit incense. I walk the rows
    from Chinese graves to where my tata rests.
I walk grandparent to grandparent in Phoenix.
        We brought the body to the house, I remember
    him once telling me about the dead & vigils
for them—*so viejas*, he said, *could pray rosary*.

Like old rotary phones, I thought: each bead
        round & numinous with number—a direct line
    to heaven. Oy ear Oy yes Oy ya—a caldo knocked
the first time I held the string with my nana
        to pull prayer as if trawling. No boat, no gunwale—
    only morning dishes yolk-streaked, a skillet
cockeyed where drained fat jellied. Same grease
        yellowed my fingers greasing my Hail Mary.
    Still, prayer's pace stalled & staggered in litany—
not knowing the words, I hung back to echo hers.

When Ng Ng died, the day of the funeral,
  a cousin stayed behind to unmake the beds,
 to sit at the door & keep the threshold swept.
So the dead don't come home by accident,
  my father said. Then, as later when he passed,
 we ate our Werther's & pocketed the quarter,
the exchange rate of sweet for the bitter
  that had me thinking of the bright, tiered rows
 beneath his register—Jawbreakers, Now
& Laters, Paydays & suckers like sapphires.

I once called my dad about the beef tongue
        he butchered & sold for the family shop—
    he'd Sharpie TONGUE & LENGUA with the price
per pound, then stake the nameplate's pin
            in the bright meat. A "born-here" boy, he didn't read
        or write the strokes, but he knew the Spanish
& Toisanese, while I know how my tata
        preferred it with pride over any filet mignon;
    how too the word sits inside *belong*—bright
& Latinate in the butcher glass of the verb.

I wondered at the stroke order of tongue,
      what mark is made first. Online, I watched ink
    fill the hollowed-out word & then pushed play
to hear it said aloud. The Toisanese sounds
      like *lee* or *leave.* I remember the beef round
    in the one-bulb light of our walk-in, the thin
windbreaker my father wore over his apron
      & the shrill sound as he sharpened his knives.
    My father's cuts were calligraphy too.
What ink print would his butcher block make?

There are streets of fillet steak & roast beef
             & streets of skirt & intestine. At the graves,
         I'd ask my dad about the Chinese dead.
Invariably, he knew them & could recite
             their family stores with their street address:
         Yee Sing on East Washington, the Wong's
H & W on Jefferson, the Ong's New Valley
             & the Mah's Sunland, both on Buckeye.
         Walking the graves alongside my father
was walking to those corner stores again.

Bank of Universal, Bank of Paradise, Bank
       of Heaven: paper money burns beside
    hibachis grilling asada at grave sites—
alchemies across the fire wire with gift
          remittance. Sending his U.S. army checks
       by way of Chinatown herbalists, Yeh Yeh
kept his mess cook soldiering secret.
          Ng Ng, unaware until she was war bride,
       came across carrying their correspondence
redolent with licorice root & ginseng.

My nana mourns in the Spanish word luto.
      I hear Orpheus with his hollow-bodied,
    plucked-string instrument tuned at ratios
equivalent to the vast & charted distances
        between planets. What if I brought butcher's
    twine to my dead to truss & tune to tongues?
—Deus—Deos—Dejos—Dios—Joss —
      What novitiate would I make? What rosary
    in pidgin prayer composed of barker's call
that haggles the strained echo of etymology?

The ear's yearning, oír in memoir: Ng Ng,
        Yeh Yeh, Nana y Tata—the syllables like
    teething stones, a necklace of mnemonics
so not to lose place. I hear, too, scissors—
        the hinge's chit, wren's song in Tata's hand.
    In the service, he often told us, he learned
to barber. A toalla over my small shoulders,
        I peered from the stool into his kit bag:
    straight razor, lather brush, jar of pomade—
his *Tres Flores*: nettle, yucca, rosemary.

NOTES

Radio circuit symbols and much of the early history of radio and radio circuitry are taken from the 1954 book *The Boy's First Book of Radio and Electronics* by Alfred Morgan.

"Teléfono Roto": For more about Motorola, toxic dumping, and the Superfund site in Phoenix, Arizona, see Andrew Ross's *Bird on Fire: Lessons from the World's Least Sustainable City.*

"Code Switches" quotes Cherríe Moraga from her essay "La Güera," collected in *This Bridge Called My Back: Writings by Radical Women of Color,* edited by Moraga and Gloria Anzaldúa.

"Raspadas": For the history of Cesar Chávez's hunger strike and Dolores Huerta's activism in Phoenix, see Rick Tejada-Flores and Gayanne Fietinghoff's documentary film *Sí Se Puede!* The shaved ice treat is more commonly gendered masculine and written *raspados.* However, curiously, in my family the word has always been said with the feminine ending, *raspadas.*

"Fuchi": For more on semiconductor production, toxic hazards, and so-called clean rooms, see "The Core: Work and the Struggle to Make a Living without Dying" in David Naguib Pellow and Lisa Sun-Hee Park's book *The Silicon Valley of Dreams: Environmental Injustice, Immigrant Workers, and the High-Tech Global Economy.*

"Twin Plants" references the documentary *Maquilapolis* by the filmmakers Sergio de la Torre and Vicky Funari. The poem is indebted to Alicia Gaspar de Alba's chapter "Poor Brown Female: The Miller's Compensation" in *Making a Killing: Femicide, Free Trade, and La Frontera* edited by Gaspar de Alba and Georgina Guzmán.

"Sirenas Del Aire, 1958" refers to the photomontage by the photographer Lola Álvarez Bravo. In regards to Homer's Sirens, the poem draws from the translation and commentary of Emily Wilson.

"Tattoo": For more on housing segregation and covenants in Phoenix, check out journalist Kaila White's reporting "Did Phoenix Ever Segregate Where Minorities Could Live?" on the podcast *Valley 101*.

"Shainadas" owes a debt to the scholar and poet Alfred Arteaga, specifically his writings on José Montoya in the book *Chicano Poetics: Heterotexts and Hybridities*.

"Half" draws upon Ilona Katzew's *Casta Painting: Images of Race in Eighteenth-Century Mexico*. The poem refers to specific paintings and descriptions included in Katzew's book.

"Antennae" references the work of Tejana composer Pauline Oliveros and draws from the work of Douglas Kahn's chapter "Pauline Oliveros: Sonosphere" in *Earth Sound Earth Signal: Energies and Earth Magnitude in the Arts*.

"Resistors": In September 2020, Amber Ortega and Nellie Jo David stopped border wall construction in southern Arizona, near Quitobaquito Springs, by peacefully obstructing the bulldozing vehicles. The epigraph comes from Ryan Devereaux's article "Indigenous Activists Arrested and Held Incommunicado Following Border Wall Protest," published in *The Intercept*.

"Super Mercado Lee Hou" refers to the histories of Mexican repatriation in the United States and anti-chino violence in Mexico. The poem owes a debt to Francisco E. Balderrama's *Decade of Betrayal: Mexican Repatriation in the 1930s*; Jason Oliver Chang's *Anti-Chinese Racism in Mexico, 1880–1940*; and Julian Lim's *Porous Borders: Multiracial Migrations and the Law in the U.S.-Mexico Borderlands*

The poem "Novena" borrows the line "There are streets of fillet steak & roast beef & streets of skirt & intestine" from John Berger's *A Seventh Man*.

ACKNOWLEDGMENTS

I am grateful to the editors and staff of the following publications in which excerpts of this book, often in earlier versions, first appeared: *Hayden's Ferry Review*, *Plume*, *New England Review*, *Paris Review*, *Poetry Northwest*, *Poetry International*, *The Nation*, *Poetry Magazine*, *The Baffler*, *Literary Hub*, and *Prairie Schooner*.

Thank you to the following editors and curators for including my work in their visions and projects. The poem "Chino" was included in the museum exhibition Soul Mining, curated by Julio César Morales and Xiaoyu Weng. "Close Reading" was selected by Eduardo C. Corral for the Academy of American Poets series Poem-a-Day. "Teléfono Roto" appeared in *Book of Curses*, a special issue of *Asian American Literary Review* edited by Lawrence-Minh Bùi Davis and Mimi Khúc. The poem "Shainadas" was selected by Paisley Rekdal for *Best American Poetry 2020*.

I am immensely thankful to the communities at Civitella Raineri and Lighthouse Works for fellowships that provided space, time, and nourishment to write. I also wish to express gratitude for generous support from UC San Diego, and to thank my amazing colleagues.

Thank you to Gerald Maa and everyone at University of Georgia Press for your support and for your belief in this project. Thank you to Maribeth Bandas and Jon Davies for your meticulous editorial work.

For their continued friendship, insight, support, and encouragement throughout the making of this book, sincere thanks to Christopher Santiago, Ari Banias, Stacey Waite, Arash Saedinia, Kathryn Walkiewicz, Ari Larissa Heinrich, Jason Bacasa, Solmaz Sharif, Josh Rivkin, Erin Beeghly, francine j. harris, Stan Mir, and Carolina Maugeri.

Forever gratitude and love to my family, with special thanks to my nana, my ai gu, and my mother, for their love, guidance, and teachings.

My deepest love and gratitude to Janelle and Gus.

GEORGIA REVIEW BOOKS

What Persists: Selected Essays on Poetry from The Georgia Review, *1988–2014*,
by Judith Kitchen

Conscientious Thinking: Making Sense in an Age of Idiot Savants,
by David Bosworth

Stargazing in the Atomic Age, by Anne Goldman

Divine Fire, poems by David Woo

Hong Kong without Us: A People's Poetry, edited by the Bauhinia Project

Hysterical Water, poems by Hannah Baker Saltmarsh

This Impermanent Earth: Environmental Writing from The Georgia Review,
edited by Douglas Carlson and Soham Patel

GAZE BACK, poems by Marylyn Tan

Natural History, poems by José Watanabe, translated by Michelle Har Kim

The Harm Fields, poems by David Lloyd

Tripas, poems by Brandon Som

Printed in the USA
CPSIA information can be obtained
at www.ICGtesting.com
CBHW030234100224
4249CB00003B/121

9 780820 363509